Fred and Jen Get Fit

by Dennis Fertig
illustrated by Meryl Henderson

Practice Decodable 32

McGraw Hill Education

Bothell, WA • Chicago, IL • Columbus, OH • New York, NY

MHEonline.com

Send all inquiries to:
McGraw-Hill Education
8787 Orion Place
Columbus, OH 43240

ISBN: 978-0-02-145345-0
MHID: 0-02-145345-4

Printed in China

8 9 10 11 12 DSS 27 26 25 24 23

Can Fred help Jen get fit?

Fred dipped a bit.

Jen dipped a bit.

Fred jogged.
Next, Jen jogged.

Fred stepped up.
Jen stepped up.

Fred hopped a bit.
Jen hopped a bit.

Fred sat down and rested.

Jen did not rest. Jen flipped.